A GUIDE FOR NEW INVESTORS IN THE STOCK MARKET

STOCKS, TIPS, AND STOCK MARKET DIPS

by Delia Williams

Delia Williams

Copyright © 2018 Delia Williams

All rights reserved.

ISBN-13: 978-1727382099

ISBN-10: 1727382099

Published by It's All About Him Media & Publishing
PO Box 850
Paw Creek, NC 28130
www.aahmp.com
980-522-8096

Edited by Delisa Rodgers-Fields
Cover design: Delisa Rodgers-Fields

Printed in the United States of America.
All rights reserved under International Copyright Law.
Contents and/or cover may not be reproduced in whole or in part in any form without the express written consent of the publisher.

DEDICATION

You know another investment book sound like blah huh? But not this time! I dedicate this book to my wonderful readers. Now start reading this book and go invest in the stock market after it like a boss!

TABLE OF CONTENTS

- Introduction — XI
- My Seed Launched Me Into The Deep — 1
- Where It All Started — 5
- Giving It Your All — 12
- False Evidence Appearing Real — 15
- Clear The Pathway For The Winners To Arrive — 25
- The Power Of A Changed Mind — 40
- Do Not Place All Your Eggs In One Basket — 46
- It Is Going To Cost You Something — 53

ACKNOWLEDGMENTS

I have to start by thanking Jesus, my Lord, and Savior. I am grateful to God for giving me the ability to write this book and experience my investment journey.

I am especially thankful for my children Tanihya, Zechariah, and Mackenzie.

Thanks to my mom, Dorothy, and father, David. I cannot express in words the love, patience, gratitude, and support you have had for me during this journey. I love both of you dearly. Also, to my siblings, thank you.

To my Apostle, Delisa Fields, and Pastor, Charmaine Johnson. I am thankful for the love, correction, and support.

To my friend, Coya, who has tremulously supported me. Thank you for always believing in me. I thank you for sowing into my vision.

Many thanks to the individuals on The Winner's Circle and my favorite secret group for the love, support, drive, and for pushing me when I was crying on the inside. Thank you for the feedback on days when I wanted to give up on my investment journey. Everyone has played a significant role in my process.

Professional Advice Disclaimer:

This book is for educational purposes only. Any opinions expressed therein are not created, sponsored, contributed to, or endorsed by financial institutions or companies. All information provided does not constitute recommendations for investments. In addition to this, the author doesn't make any guarantee as for results for investment opinions or suggestions.

No person should make any investment decision(s) without first consulting their own financial advisor and conducting their own personal research. This information contains general advice that has not been tailored for your own particular situations. The author is not liable for any financial loss from information this book. Investment products are not FDIC insured. Investing involves substantial risk.

Delia Williams

Introduction

This book is a simple guide to introduce individuals to the stock market and tips related to it. In fact, most people want to learn more about the stock market, but fear of not understanding the stock marketplaces a halt in their decision. *Stocks, Tips, and Stock Market Dips* is essential today for many reasons, to say the least, this book provides an insight on the stock market from a single mother's perspective who experienced significant losses in her life. After discovering her life's purpose, she was given a revelation to understand the mysteries of the stock market.

In this book, you will learn the history of the stock market and tips for how it operates. You will learn how I started investing with less than $1,000. This book will also provide insight on how to work towards financial freedom and legacy building. Sit back as I invite you into my life and how the stereotypical financial investment market is about to dominated by the average "Joe's" or "Jane's," like you and me.

Through my love of the stock market, I successfully learned stock market tips that I am about to share with you. My investment knowledge will be revealed to you in an easy to understand format.

Some people want to know how long does it take to be successful in the stock market? I believe this is a great question. Being successful in the stock market depends on you! Take a moment to define success for some individual's success may be paying their bills on time; for others, it could be having $200.00 extra dollars after they have spent all of their money on bills, or it can be making $10,000 per month. Success does not always need to have a digital number attached to it.

What does success look like? Does success have a financial dollar amount attached to it? If so, what is that amount you will need to be successful? I believe being successful in the stock market will depend on your mindset, ability to change your financial habits, willingness to learn about the stock market, reading, listening to podcasts/videos/seminars, and implementing financial investment strategies.

I did not invent the stock market or rules related to it. I created a financial plan, followed an investor guru, and waited patiently. Many individuals believe you need thousands of dollars to invest in the stock market, but that is far from the truth. I believe my readers will improve their understanding of the stock market, prepare an action plan, and work diligently towards their financial independence.

CHAPTER ONE

 My Seed Launched Me Into The Deep

I didn't invent the stock market or rules for financial success. Many people believe they need thousands or millions of dollars to successfully invest in the stock market. I did not start with hundreds of thousands of dollars as many financial advisors recommend. I started with the money I had left over from my retirement account. I decided to aggressively invest my retirement funds in an investment account. At the time, I did not know what I was doing until I received an email from the investment firm about withdrawals made on my account.

My initial journey started after I sowed the largest seed in my life which was a $1,000. You see, I worked in a professional setting for several years. I received several degrees including a Master's, but there was a void deep inside. I did not realize that sowing my $1,000 seed pushed me into purpose and destiny. I am a firm believer in sowing and reaping. Jesus blessed me in a significant way. After being fired from my job, Jesus sustained me. I moved to another state, started my own investment education business, and shared the good news about what Jesus did in my life to individuals near and far.

By faith, I believed Jesus would break the spirit of poverty from affecting my children by sowing the $1,000 seed between two churches. I grew up in poverty. I did not want my children or grandchildren to experience living without Jesus or live a strapped financial lifestyle. I placed my trust in Jesus to honor my financial seed to do a new thing in my children's life. I decided the spirit of poverty, lack, and not having enough was stopping with me.

After I received a message in reference to withdrawals from my investment account, I was curious to know how this could happen. My account superseded the $1,000 seed I sowed by the thousands. I was ecstatic.

After leaving your job by force or choice, did you spend the money remaining in your retirement account? If, so why? This is a simple question for you. You needed your money, right? Trust me; I did this as well in the past; however, I discovered there was a problem. It was me and the way I thought about money. I knew that if I withdrew the money I made by aggressively investing in the stock market, I would spend it. I did not have any understanding about the stock market or what to do with the money. I most definitely would have purchased some clothes or new pairs of shoes. I decided to do some research.

I made a rational decision to reinvest the money into the stock market. During my time researching the stock market, I came across a conference in Atlanta, GA. I attended this stock market investor's conference presented by a well-known hedge fund manager.

My journey continued after this conference to learn, read, and teach individuals how to invest in the stock market. Information about the stock market did not come to me right away even after I attended the conference. I did not review the information for weeks. I had brain overload. The information I received was sounding like blah, blah, and blah! I decided to learn about the stock market one day at a time.

Do you learn best by reading, viewing a video, a combination of both, or someone teaching you in person? You have to develop a learning strategy that will work best for you.

CHAPTER TWO

Where It All Started

The stock market can seem to be an intimidating word. When you think about the stock market, what comes to your mind? Taboo, Blah, or "Oh no, a Market CRASH," or losing all my money?

Let's set the record straight and talk about the myths of the stock market. You may have heard investing in the stock market is for rich people. If so, that is a lie. How about the myth of investing in the stock market is too hard? The statement is far from the truth. Now, how about this myth that big companies are the only ones to make money in the stock market. I want to know and have a clear understanding that investing in the stock market does come with highs and lows. Some highs in the stock market can include making a lot of money in the stock and receiving knowledge of it. A low point in the stock market is an investor losing some or all of their money. Notwithstanding, with hard work and dedication, you can achieve the success story just like any other financial investor guru.

The stock market can be frightening for a person who is not a part of the financial industry. A notable event can affect and cause the stock market to soar or plunge. Some significant events in the history of impacting the stock market include a presidential election, recession, corporate fraud or scandal within companies, declaration of war, hurricanes, or housing crises. These are some of the many events that shaped the history of the stock market in America. For example, the Great Depression played a significant role in the stock market falling dramatically. During this timeframe, the United States economy was affected for about ten years. Extreme fear, whenever a monumental shift in the economy occurs in the world, may add fuel to the fire and result in the stock market dropping significantly at an alarming rate.

Always remember supply and demand. The stock market has a supply and demand rule just like other organizations. When investing, consider the laws of supply and demand as it relates to the stock market. Consider also the economic situation, its data, interest rates, and data from other corporations. The demands of stocks may occur when the economic climate is performing well. As a result, the demand for stocks will be high.

The economy has always played an essential role in the supply and demand of purchasing or selling stocks. Would you buy a stock if the economy is performing poorly? This is a question that needs to be answered. This question separates the best from the rest. For example, a temporary situation can cause a difference in companies that are selling and consumers who are purchasing. *Buy in fear and sell in greed* is a catchphrase used in the stock market as a way to sell and buy stocks, bonds, etc.

The stock market can be frightening because of the fear of the unknown. There are rules to the stock market which among them is not to lose money. Another rule is for you to create a financial investment plan. As a potential or new investor, you may want to invest in a company that you are familiar with, and that offers products you use on a daily basis. A person usually draws back from what they do not understand. If you have never bob-sleighed, why would you invest in the company that markets those products?

If you were able to understand the stock market, would you invest in it? As a potential or new investor, you have to make time to correctly understand the stock market. Using proper research tools and discovering economic indicators can determine when a person should invest in the stock market. Your goal should not be to attempt to time the stock market or the performance of it.

The stock market was created to sell and buy stocks, bonds, mutual funds, ETF's, and other investment securities. The goal of the stock market is to generate revenue for corporations. It is that simple. For example, you can spend fifteen minutes a day by listening to the podcast, reading, or watching training/teaching videos on the stock market. The history of the stock market began in

Philadelphia, PA. The Philadelphia Stock Exchange (PHLX) is one of the oldest stock market exchanges in the history of the United States. Currently, PHLX has a trading floor and electronic services for investment securities to be purchased and sold.

There are two stock exchanges in the United States which are: New York Stock Exchange (NYSE) and National Association of Securities Dealers Automated Quotations exchange (NASDAQ). The NASDAQ allows individuals to sell and purchase bonds, stocks, mutual funds, ETF's and other investment securities by an online stock market exchange. The NASDAQ has over 3,000 stocks listed. The NASDAQ is the second largest exchange stock market available online. Location is the difference between the NYSE and NASDAQ.

The NYSE is a stock exchange market and rumored to be the largest exchange in the world. The NYSE trades around 2,800 companies. Individuals can purchase or sell investment securities such as a stock, bond, ETF's, index, mutual funds, etc. on the NYSE. The NYSE stock exchange is a physical location in which you may be familiar with it by the famous "Wall Street." At this location, stockbrokers can purchase or sell investment securities.

The NASDAQ is an online stock exchange where stockbrokers can buy and sell investment securities. The stock market was created for companies to raise capital. Companies are able to "go public" by releasing an initial public offering (IPO) for investors to buy shares in their company to raise money without them going into debt. Going public is a stock market term that allows individuals in the public to invest in the stock market. A share represents part ownership in a company. A stock also represents a percentage of the company's assets and earnings. Now that you know why the stock market was created, it should not seem as intimidating.

How you ever heard of the Dow Jones or the S & P 500? Both of them are American indexes used in the stock market for analysts, stock brokers, etc. to measure how the stock market is doing. The Dow Jones, which is also known as the Dow Jones Industrial Average (DIJA), is a stock market index with thirty companies that are traded for investors to purchase on the New York Stock Exchange (NYSE). Some notable companies included in the DIJA are Apple Inc., The Coca-Cola Company, Exxon Mobil Corporation, and Nike, Inc. As of August 2018, the DIJA current price is listed around $25,415. Remember, as the market changes, so will the prices in stock market investment securities.

The S & P 500 is a stock market index which also stands for The Standard & Poor's 500. There are around 500 company stocks listed in the S & P 500. This index is used to check the performance of large-cap American companies. The S & P 500 can also be viewed as a representation of the entire stock market. You may have heard of companies such as Alphabet (GOOG), Microsoft Corp (MSFT), Facebook Inc. (FB), or Footlocker (FL) which are all a part of the S & P 500. The current price for the S&P 500 as of August 2018, is around $2,816.

CHAPTER THREE

Giving It Your All

The first tip is for investors to do their homework when investing in the stock market. When I say do your homework, I am referring to learning about the business you are about to purchase. Your first goal should be to invest in a company you are already familiar with. Take a few minutes to look around your home. Which type of products is in your house? Which type of vehicle do you drive? Are you with team Apple or team Android? Do you wear eyeglasses or contacts? Which grade of fuel do you use in your car?

The second tip to use as a rule of thumb is when learning about the stock market, buy in fear and sell in greed as mentioned. Many investors use this simple approach to purchase and sell investment securities in the stock market. Investors must learn when to purchase a stock, mutual funds, indexes, or investment security. When other investors are driven by fear of the stock market dropping, you can develop a plan to purchase investments that are undervalued. Before you decide to purchase an investment security, must you do your homework?

Low stock prices do not necessarily mean the company is a wonderful business to invest your money. Create an investment strategy that will work best for you and your family. If you create a plan, it is simple to follow it. When you have a plan, it allows you to stay on track to meet your future goals. If you fail to plan, then you fail to plan. Get your investment strategy simple. Be concerned but unconcerned at the same time with all the financial chaos reported on the news about the stock market. It is essential not to allow your emotions to control your investing decisions. A simple approach will let you to be prepared and ready to recognize mistakes or lousy investment. Also, you can easily adjust how long you should hold or sell investment securities.

If you were able to answer any of these questions, have a potential list of companies that you are familiar with. I always tell my students you know more about investing than you give yourself credit for. Now, that you have a list of companies, you need to research the companies to determine if it is a great company to invest in. Remember to buy damaged stocks not damaged companies. There are several ways to determine if a stock is damaged. Several ways to assess it is if an event happened to cause the shares (stocks) to decrease in value.

CHAPTER FOUR

False Evidence Appearing Real

What is fear? Fear is false evidence appearing real. The first tip to overcome fear in the stock market is to educate yourself about it. When you understand the stock market, you can learn what to watch for and how to successfully purchase and sell investment securities.

The stock market is like a moody person. You should not be emotional as well. The stock market fluctuates throughout the day as stockbrokers are selling and purchasing investment securities for corporations and individual investors. Whenever a person understands the stock market, they can be less apprehensive about it.

Another way to reduce anxiety is by creating an entrance and exit plan. I always tell my students to purchase investment securities that you are capable of understanding. Why invest in Ski Company if you do not understand anything about it? Why should you invest in Cigarette Company if you despise tobacco products? Invest in companies that match our values and stands for what we believe in. One of your main goals should be to read, to read, and to read more books about the stock market from guru investors.

The second tip is to look at your end goals. Do not invest money in the stock market that you need now. Set goals, re-evaluate, and focus on your game plan.

You can invest your money better than any other financial institution. Once you understand how to properly invest your money. Take control of your investment accounts by learning about the stock market, developing a financial plan, and using strategies that best fit the needs of your family's situation. Start investing in small amounts until you can get the swing of things. I believe investment terms and jargon are meant to confuse you. Your goal should not be to get rich. Set a realistic goal to take control of your money and become financially stable.

I always ask my students to understand their why?

What is your *why*? My why is related to my generation living in poverty and not understanding or learning about finances. My *why* looks at me in the face every day which is my three children. My *why* relates to a population of people who are being taken advantage of by financial advisors.

When researching your potential business, you may want to consider: the name of the company, the industry (healthcare, retail, etc.), the stock symbol, the cost per share, and the stock symbol. Ask yourself will the company be listed in your short, medium, or long-term plan?

Take the time and tell me who can manage your money better than you? Okay, you may have had financial difficulties in the past. You may have come from a generation of people who mismanage money but what if you are the first investor in your family? Guess what? So, am I! If I was able to successfully learn about the stock market, so can you. A person may think no one has ever learned how to manage money properly or how to invest in many types of investments securities. If that person is you, this is the time to take control of your life. I have faith in you. I believe by faith you are stronger than what you appear to be.

Don't allow doubt and fear to take control of your life so you will not be financially free. Without taking a risk, you will not have a reward. I believe being afraid in the stock market is related to poor understanding. It is essential to learn about the stock market so you can become less fearful of it. So, what is the fear about? The anxiety in the stock market can be related to losing all of your money. If this is the case, I can understand why a person would not want to invest in the stock market.

Another problem related to the stock market is politics. I believe politics can have an influence on the stock market by governmental policies. A policy can impact an individual's taxes or growth in an economy. So yes, governmental policies can exacerbate the fear individuals have in the stock market.

Throughout my time teaching individuals how to invest in the stock market, I noticed there is a fear related to a person investing in the stock market as an individual as opposed to a company doing it for them. I believe the fear of someone investing your money for you should be scarier than doing it yourself. Who can invest your money better than you? Listen, this is what you should understand; investing in the stock market is simple. Do not become fearful about the stock market by listening to fancy words, and watching the suits, dresses, and shoes. Some financial advisors are paid by their employer to sell investment products to you. Do you believe they have the time to teach you about obtaining investment products? You have to decide to control your money rather than allow another person to control it. I believe as a new investor that it will be wise to learn about the stock market and how the market works.

In most cases, the financial advisor's goals are to sell you their investment products and make a commission. I had the excellent opportunity to meet a financial advisor after opening my investment account. This individual did not take the time to ask about my financial goals or recommend any investment products. After the advisor reviewed my financial statement, he was disinterested in assisting me. Apparently, I did not have enough money in my account for him to receive a commission from selling a mutual fund or other investment security to me.

Nevertheless, I seemed to spark his interest when I mentioned funds that needed to be transferred from another company to my account. I was uninterested in his assistance after I was treated like that. I was a new investor and had a desire to learn and improve my financial situation.

Under any circumstances, I was willing to learn about the stock market. My goal is to teach to individuals what I have learned about the stock market so they can invest their money themselves. There are many people in your local community and around the world who have the desire to invest in the stock market but are afraid to do so. You have a 50/50 chance when investing in the stock market. You have a chance to lose money and learn from your mistakes and regroup. You also have an opportunity to earn money by choosing the right investment securities. What if you never learn to invest in the stock market? How are you going to reach your financial goals?

I am one of the first investors in my family who understand the stock market and am willing to share information with the public. My financial investment learning experience started when I was a child. Reflecting on this, I called this experience *financial seeds* that were planted by my oldest brother, Gerard and his grandmother. I remember my brother won the stock market challenge during his high school years. I had the opportunity to witness him bring home a plaque which is still at my mother's house. Everyone was excited.

I also recall when my brothers received money from bonds that their grandmother had established. I didn't know then, but now I understand that their grandmother purchased an investment security which was a *bond*. My brothers received money from the interest of the bonds every year, and they received the money after the maturity date. I remember my brothers smiling and joking about items they were going to purchase after cashing in their bond certificates which came on a regular basis up until adulthood. By the way, I was extremely jealous. Heck yeah, I wanted a check as well.

Now, I realize the need of investing at an early can be beneficial to you and your family. Purchasing a bond certificate can be useful to assist your children, relatives, friends, or organization with college, startup business fees, vacations, etc. Every year on the maturity date of the bond issue date, my brothers received a check. I guess that was unfair for me watching them spend their investment money on a yearly basis.

As I child, I related the stock market to my brother receiving bonds in the mailbox and other family members' retirement plans. Does relating the stock market to retirements plan sound like blah? This could be because a retirement plan alone may not satisfy your financial goals after you retire. It is sad to think about individuals who've worked their entire life and cannot live without having a financial burden after they retire. Most people have to continue to work after they retire to meet their financial needs with the rate of inflation. The full retirement age in America is 67.

A person can retire early at the age of 62. Think about your retirement goals. How are you going to reach them? Do you plan on working a job that you most likely could care less about until the age of 67? If you invest in your employer's retirement plan, then you have one foot in the door. However, do you understand your employer's plan?

Most individuals in my family have found their form of financial security in retirement plans such as 401k, 403b, TSP Plans or IRAs. I often noticed individuals believe their retirement plan is going to give us the financial freedom we dream of. But guess what? Please think again.

The average African American family may retire with $19,000. A white family retires with an average of $130,000 in their retirement accounts.

On the other hand, a Hispanic family's retirement accounts may average $12,000. Seems kind of unfair? There is a significant wealth gap between racial groups.

CHAPTER FIVE
Clear The Path For The Winner To Arrive

A false reality can be planted in our heads by not paying attention to our financial goals. I did not have any famous or successful individuals that make money because of the stock market or as an investor. As a child, success was related to going to college, receiving a degree, and retiring when you are in your 60's. Successful people appeared to be individuals who were far away on television, playing sports, or acting in a movie.

My understanding of success as a child was not related to stock market investing. Through observation, I realize my race is far behind in investing in the stock market. The average African American family retires from their career with less than a year of living wages in their retirement account. Some of us tend to live in a false reality of what our life should or could be. I have noticed that throughout my years of having similar thoughts and lived a precarious financial lifestyle.

I remember going to the stores purchasing the latest in the most fabulous items such as Nike Air Jordan's, expensive handbags, ordering takeout rather than cooking, or spending a lot of money on my hair. I purchased $160.00 for some shoes. Also, I paid more than $200.00 for someone to braid my hair with the extensions. I held myself accountable for my negative financial habits. I had to repent for mismanaging my money. To change your financial situation, we should become aware of our habits.

Some members in the African American community have been left behind regarding investing in the stock market. If you feel like that is you, then it is time to start investing in your financial future. I believe a person who has a poverty mindset can be a barrier to your success. Having a poverty mindset does not necessarily means the person is living in poverty. Also, there can be some social, and emotional challenges related to poverty among the African American community.

I experienced being without a house, car, and money. I have lived paycheck to paycheck. I have lived with a lot and with less. I have purchased material items without making a rational decision. I have bought tangible things instead of paying my bills. I had to hold myself accountable because I was spending money I did not have.

I remember hearing family members using and saying the famous catchphrase that many of us grew up hearing, "Robbing Peter to pay Paul." In my community, this catchphrase simply to take from one area to use it in another area. There were individuals who believed this was a way to live.

I believed the same thing while growing up. There is no fun when working to pay your bills and being unable to go out to a movie, to dinner, or go skating or bowling. We have to push past the stigma associated with just having enough and being ok with that. You have to learn about money, use wise choices with our money, and live an abundant lifestyle.

I believe in working to make an honest living; however, the catchphrase, "Robbing Peter to pay

Paul," that I heard as a child was following behind me years later. A part of that was because I believed in it. I am not proud of living paycheck to paycheck. I am also not proud of taking from one source to use in another area. It was truly embarrassing. I noticed individuals in my family depending entirely on social security and disability funds to help them make ends meet after retirement.

I talked to many individuals in the African America community who have a hard time paying off debt and saving money. I believe some of our financial habits are generational but what are we doing to change it? You must hold yourself accountable for not investing in yourself and learning more about finances. You should also examine your own motive for purchasing materialistic items and not properly saving or budgeting your money.

Tip One in investing is to *Understand Your Why*. Do you know why you want to invest? To understand your why is wrapped into your purpose and values.

Take a few minutes to sit back and define your purpose and what you believe in. *Understanding you're why* requires you to dig deep. Now is the time to determine what success means to you. What does success look like? Completing these few questions will move you closer to your purpose in life. You should always remember your why.

My purpose in life started after I discovered my why. When I discovered my *why*, it allowed me to live again and walk on purpose. I realized the winner has always lived inside of me. The winner was hiding until purpose and destiny came knocking on the door in my life. It was time for the winner that lived inside of me all of these years to rise and take control of her life and financial situation.

I started to seek the Lord and trust Him. In my quiet time, I would listen to the Lord and write in my journal. I often would chat with the Lord in my private time, you know like a friend. I have chats with the Lord like that. There were some things in my life I wanted to know. I started to seek the Lord by praying, fasting, worshiping and reading. He answered of course in His perfect timing. There were mysteries the Lord revealed to me after I dedicated my life to Jesus and walked on a mission to fulfill His will for my life.

If you want to invest to get rich, you will be chasing money your entire life. Investing in the stock market is not a get rich quick scheme. Let's say your why is to get rich and when you become rich, what is your game plan? After you purchase homes, get cars out of debt, make donations, bless family members and or friends, pay tithes, and schedule vacations, now what? Some individuals go through life focusing on daily activities, family, and careers. As the days pass by, we tend to feel as if we are not getting ahead. Whenever you discover your purpose, you will find a new meaning to live.

Do not allow your *why* to be based upon completing "a thing" or money. If your why is based upon money, you will be chasing money your entire life. Of course, we need money for material items. You must discover what is really important in your life. Always understand everyone's *why* for they are pursuing their dreams and purpose in life and it will be different; that is ok. Discover your purpose and understanding your why and the money will come.

Tip Two is to believe in you. If you do not believe in yourself, who will? I believe you can become a great investor with hard work, patience, reading, and listening. Believing in yourself should not be based on other people's opinions about you. It can be hard to believe in financial freedom when the odds are against you. I have many odds against me, but I still believe I can do it. You must fully believe in yourself and your ability to achieve success. It is a must to believe in you which is my secret as well.

Another secret I use to learn about the stock market is *coat-tailing*. The term refers to following a guru and learning from them. I have two guru investors whom I follow. I do understand I may not have millions of shares in companies at this present time; however, by using the coat-tailing method and developing a plan, I started to see the light in the dark tunnel. I performed research of the investors and learned from them. Do I understand that everything they are doing will not work in my favor? Heck yeah, I do! It is essential to gather small nuggets of information from various sources and use them to help you along your journey. For example, throughout my stock investment journey, I would check out one of my favorite guru's investment portfolios. You can have a favorite investor as well. Take a few minutes to research a great stock market investor online. Does that investor match your values, etc.? Make sure you are able to access their investment portfolio online. Also, take some notes of their accomplishments, family values, investment strategies, and business information. After, I take a glance at their portfolio; I can determine which companies match my values and I proceed from there.

At first, learning about the stock market was hard. The stock market can be a challenge, but with hard work, reading, and patience, you can do it. I enjoy learning about the stock market and what is going on in the world. A great tip that will help you to learn more about the stock market is to watch or reach about world events. Give it your all.

If you are considering why you should invest, think

about why you shouldn't. Investing in your future is essential. Investing is a way to keep up with inflation. I am writing this book in the year, 2018.

Can you imagine how much a gallon of gas will be in 2028 or 2038? Can you image how much a gallon of milk will be? A gallon of milk may cost you around $10.00 to $15.00 during that timeframe. If that happens, I will milk the cow myself and package the milk in a bottle.

Inflation occurs as goods and services increases. If you invest your money correctly, you will be able to retire on your own terms. There are benefits to investing in the stock market which includes ownership in a successful business, money, of course, and diversification or receiving quarterly dividend income.

A person should invest in the stock market to reach their financial goals such as purchasing a new car, vacation, saving for college, house, or retirement. I love to say you have to be able to make sense out of nonsense. If the stock market is similar to listening to an unfamiliar language, it is a great way to make sense out of it. Also, you can create weekly goals to educate yourself by watching, listening, or reading from stock market-related news on CNN Money, Yahoo Finance, Seeking Alpha, podcasts, newspapers, magazines such as *Barron's*, or *The Wall Street Journal*. These are some investment researching examples among hundreds that are available for you as well.

Investing in the stock market become simple after receiving education about it. I believe having a negative mindset about money can be a learned behavior. To reduce this mindset, you need to recognize that behavior.

You have to understand there are a lot of rich people who have a poor mindset. I often think about people who win the lottery. It is cool to think about winning the lottery by doing nothing. Sure, you gave the cashier $1, $5, or $100 to win this large sum of money. But are you able to manage 100 million dollars? I want to know if you were able to maintain the money you had on your job; let's say $2,000, $5,000, or $10,000. How can you possibly manage

$100 million if you can't handle $1,000?

Often, the winners of the lottery appear to have less money at the end of their spending spree. I do agree that the lottery changes their lives. The change that occurred in their lives was not in a good way. As for myself, I often focus on the result instead of the now.

Most great investors create a financial plan. In your financial plan, you should consider short, medium, and long-term goals. As a future investor, focus on your goals and purchase damaged stocks and not damaged companies. A damaged company can happen from a big event. For example, a security breach in customer personal data or outbreak with meat or dairy products can create a decreased in the value of the stock. You need to note that in this example, you would be purchasing a damaged stock and not a damaged business.

The goal of investing is to place your money in an account with an expectation of receiving a profit. Investing can be viewed as a vehicle. The vehicle itself is empty until investment securities are placed inside of it. For example, a share of stock(s) is on your passenger side. Bonds, Exchange Traded Funds (ETFs), or mutual funds all can be placed in your vehicle as back seat passengers. You can invest your money yourself or have a financial investment advisor/broker do it for you. I prefer investing as an individual rather than a financial advisor doing it for me. This is so I can be in control of which type of companies I am investing.

Another form of investing is diversifying your portfolio. An investor should ensure they have a properly diversified portfolio among asset classes. A portfolio is a variety of investments. There are several types of portfolios such as conservative, moderate, and aggressive portfolios.

These three portfolios will vary according to your risk level. A conservative portfolio investor has a lower risk tolerance level. In a conservative portfolio, investors can have 80% bonds, 10% stocks, and 10% cash. A moderate portfolio can refer to an investor who has low to moderate risk. For example, a moderate portfolio can have 60% stocks, 30% bonds, and 10% cash. An aggressive portfolio may have a higher risk level in comparison to conservative or moderate portfolios. Aggressive portfolios can have 75% stocks, 20% bonds, and 5% cash. Your portfolio will be tailored to meet your financial goals.

There are some people who want to save for college, marriage, or to purchase a home. Whenever you are determining your financial investment goals, the investments that are listed in your portfolio can be created for that goal. Your portfolio can change throughout the duration of your investment journey.

What is the interest rate of your cash deposited in your local bank? Will the cash sitting in your local bank help you reach your long-term financial goals? I use cash for emergency situations and for monthly expenses. You can lose money by saving. Whenever you are considering long-term financial goals, you have to include inflation. Think of investing like this for without investing there is no risk. Also, without investing there will be no reward. You could be losing money by saving it at your local bank.

The average interest rate from a savings account in

a bank is estimated to be 0.5%; notwithstanding, this is not always the case. Some bank rates can change according to the amount of money saved in your account. There are credit unions and online banks that may offer higher interest rates. If you are the lucky group of individuals who save your money at the bank, you may receive a measly 1.00% interest rate. How are you protecting yourself from inflation? Will saving your money in your local bank save you from inflation?

When you think about investing in the stock market, you must start somewhere. You cannot continue to desire other people's lifestyle if you are unwilling to work for the lifestyle of your dreams. One useful tip I will share with you is to forget about the reasons for investing in the stock market will not work. Now, think about your *why* that is possible to make money in the stock market.

I believe the stock market was created to be intimidating. I was terrified of the stock market before learning about it. I was afraid of the unknown.

After learning about the stock market, you can

create a diversified portfolio that will be suited for your family. A great investor uses their portfolio and the investment securities in it to create the lifestyle they dream of. In a way, investing in the stock market is a great way to catch up with inflation. I want you to understand there is no guaranteed to a reward. Stocks can be volatile investment security. However, if you do not invest in the stock market, it may be difficult to obtain your financial goals.

CHAPTER SIX

The Power of a Changed Mind

Do you believe the catchphrase, "The rich get richer and the poor stay poorer?" A part of that catchphrase stems from imbalanced economic situations. There are also political reasons that include policy or laws that discriminate against certain economic classes. The middle-class population accounts for a considerable percentage in the United States. Lower income earners may not have the same access to financial education, taxes benefits, and schools as the 1% of the wealthy population in America. For this reason, economic inequality is high and financial education is rare in certain social communities, racial groups, and economic classes.

As with anything in life, you must change your mindset and believe you can achieve "a thing." The way a person grew up can play a role in how they think about money, business, careers, college, or financial investments. You must develop a positive mindset when becoming an investor. Try to think of investing in the stock market as a business. There are many mindsets when it comes to investing.

The first mindset of potential investors is the "I can't invest in the stock market at the moment individuals." These individuals are intrigued by investing in the stock market, but their situation won't allow them to do so. This happens when you have a mindset to invest in the stock market but do not have the financial means to do so. During this time, it is essential to learn from gurus, read, listen to podcasts, and wait.

The second mindset is individuals who say, "I am too busy to invest in the stock market myself." These potential investors prefer to give their money to a financial institution or an advisor to invest for them. Some people who fall into this situation may feel like they are too busy to learn about the stock market on their own. Potential investors in this category, in this case, heed the advice from their fund manager or advisor instead of researching the information for themselves.

There are people who have no desire to invest in the stock market. Individuals with this type of mindset believe they do not have enough money to invest in the first place so why bother. A reason why individuals in this group have no desire is ignorance about financial investments. There are some people with mindsets made up in their mind that they can learn about the stock market later on in life. Having this type of mindset allows a person to live in a false reality and place materialistic things in their lives to fill a void. Therefore, a person would instead purchase materialistic items versus investing. Your mindset can influence the way you invest in the stock market. A person will start to believe what they think.

For example, if you are able to purchase stocks at a wholesale, would you buy them? Yes, course you would! Everyone loves to purchase something on sale. Now, think of stock market investing in the same aspect. Do you love McDonald's? As of August 2018, McDonald's Corp traded on the NYSE for around $153 per share. What if a significant event occurred within their corporation and caused the shares in the stock price to fall? Would you purchase shares of McDonald's stock for $75.00? I am sure you would.

Let's look at another example of McDonald's. During April 1985, the shares were $1.82. If you had 1,000 shares of stock in McDonald's in the 80's, it would have cost you around $1,800. Currently, your initial $1,800 investment would become around $153,000. The goal of making money in the stock market is a positive mindset, waiting, reading, great investment strategies, and endurance to finish your financial goals strong. A person will get out of anything from what they put in.

Create a list of the challenges you have with your mindset regarding investing. I believe having a negative mindset about investing can develop a sense of financial sabotage. One tip to overcome a negative mindset is to identify barriers that cause your mind to be cynical. You must understand that the financial investment world appears to be a top-secret world that includes the most influential people, the elite. You can be a part of this investment world after you change your mindset and believe in yourself.

Committing to change is not only a verbal decision, but you must also act as well. You can achieve your financial goals by learning a new skill and working towards your own development. We are all unique and do not learn the same way. Recognize your learning style to determine if you learn best by reading books, listening to someone speak, audiobooks, and or by demonstration. Eliminate unhealthy financial habits by starting small and making confident decisions.

In the world of investing, financial brokers and analysts may tend to offer the best investment guidance to individuals who have $100,000, $250,000, $500,000, or 1 million dollars. But what about the small people? What about the working class and middle-class individuals? You can still invest in the stock market with small amounts of money contrary to popular belief. If you have $5.00, $50.00, $100.00, or $500.00, start investing with that.

When your mind is made up to invest in the stock market, you could start by purchasing fractional shares in a company. Some investment firms allow individuals from the beginner to advanced level to purchase fractional shares. Purchasing fractional shares allow everyone the ability to invest in the stock market. Being a potential new investor, repetition is the key to success after a financial plan is created. Try not spending too much time recreating a wheel. Spend more of your time following gurus, learning about the stock market, reading, and working on a financial plan or adjusting it along the process. Investment firms that offer fractional shares are Betterment, Motif, Stash, or Stockpile. Before you start investing with fractional shares, remember to develop your investment plan and learn about the stock market.

CHAPTER SEVEN

Do Not Place All Your Eggs In One Basket

Diversification is an option some investors use in the stock market. I like to inform my students not to place all of their eggs in one basket. Diversification is a mixture of investments that may lower an investor risk. An investor can diversify their investment portfolio by purchasing stocks, bonds, mutual funds, real estate, indexes, and or exchange-traded funds (ETFs). Each financial investment industry offers a potential opportunity. There are thousands of investments to purchase or sold on the stock market exchanges. Whenever you decide to make that jump into the stock market, be sure to invest in a company you are already familiar with.

Diversification allows some investors to feel safe. An investor can diversify according to industries such as energy, real estate, financial or banking, technology, utilities, etc. Within a diversified portfolio, an investor can have mutual funds, stocks, bonds, etc. based upon their risk tolerance. Do not be afraid to start small, I did. Learn while you are starting small. Starting with small amounts of money and investments allows the investor to take their time to learn about the stock market.

Overdiversifying your portfolio is similar to placing all your eggs in one basket. If your basket falls, all your eggs will break. However, if you have multiple baskets and one basket dropped on the ground, you may have a higher chance to keep the rest of the eggs from breaking.

The stock market is like a person with mood swings. It fluctuates throughout the day; therefore, plan, plan, and plan again. The goal of investing is to place your money in an account with an expectation of receiving a profit. Think of your investment portfolio as a vehicle. The vehicle itself is empty until passengers are sitting in the seats of the car. As you can image, there is a need for investment securities in your portfolio. In this case, a share of stock(s) is on your passenger side. Bonds, exchange-traded funds (ETFs), or mutual funds all can be placed in your vehicle as back seat passengers. You are able to select various of investment securities to be "riding in your vehicle's back seat."

A tip to always remember when selecting investment securities is that they may change throughout your journey. You can invest your money yourself or have a financial investment advisor/broker do it for you. I prefer individual investing. This is so I can control the choice of companies I am investing. I can buy and sell investment securities at my own leisure.

How many stocks, bonds, ETFs, etc. you should have will depend upon you. FYI, having one bond or ETF is better than none. The goal is acquiring more investment securities in your portfolio as you learn. The risk is still present after your portfolio is diversified. If you own a lot of stocks, you may have a difficult time keeping up with them. Whenever you decide to diversify your portfolio, you should determine what is enough. In a sense, diversification can save you in the event of a bear market. Take some time to use common sense investing. Meaning, know precisely what it says and invest using your common sense. A great tip is to analyze a guru's investment portfolio to determine how diversified their positions are. The bottom line here is not to make a new wheel when there is one for you to ride on.

As a potential or new investor, diversification can be specific to an industry, country, or a company. The main point of diversification is to reduce your risk level when investing in the stock market. Keep in mind that various countries may offer a different investment selection in comparison to investing in one country. Some countries may be big on their oil industries while another has gold or rare minerals. Investing in foreign countries does come with risks as any other type of investing. Selecting the right investment securities depends upon your personal financial needs.

Stock Market Dips

A dip in the stock market can be seen as a tragic event. The stock market appears to be exciting to spectators when you hear stories that the NYSE or S&P 500 has dropped. Economic and catastrophic events I have explained in the chapter are some factors that play an essential role in the rise and fall of the stock market.

The housing market crash in 2008 took a toll on working people across America. While investors saw this as an excellent opportunity to invest in real estate, there were individuals losing their homes on a daily basis. The financial markets took a significant loss which included the mortgage and credit industries and the government bailout. I will never forget how traumatic the housing market was for families in my community and across America.

A stock market dip refers to the market that is going down, and prices are decreasing. In this case, investors may lose money. An investor refers to a dip as a *bear market*. A dip in stock can represent an opportunity for you to invest in the stock market. Some investors may see this as *timing the market*. This investment strategy is when investors follow the sales of stocks according to when there is a decrease in the prices. You should know that timing the stock market does not always pan out to be the best investment solution.

Due to the stock market and its irrational behavior tendencies, people have become emotional investors. The news has its fair share of responsibility in the role of how some emotionally people invest in the stock market. It is essential, as a future investor, not to be so caught up in the hype on television and financial advisors or analysists. Make sure you understand your potential business (stock) as a great investment opportunity. Just because a stock falls below a certain price, it does not mean it should be purchased. Some stocks listed on the stock market exchange can be overpriced.

By purchasing stocks during a dip, it can be determined you are buying a stock at a lower rate. There is a period in the stock when the stock market goes back up. When the stock market rises, it is considered to be a *bull market*. A bull market suggests that its stock prices are going or trending up. In the stock market, a bull market can represent the raising of the economy and growth within a company. All investors expect a bull market. A solid foundation in the economy causes the raising of stocks which in turn creates revenue for investors.

CHAPTER EIGHT

It Is Going To Cost You Something

Can the cost of investing be more painful than you expected it to be? It is vital to read investment books for beginners and start small. Investing is a lifestyle change. Whenever you plan to invest, it is going to cost you something. Investing requires you to be patient. You must spend money to make money, right? Yes, this is true.

I believed by receiving a Master's degree that I was exempted. Oh boy, was I wrong. Years later, I discovered the mountains of financial debt that were associated with having a degree and lack of employment opportunity in my field of expertise. Having a Master's degree did not excuse my lack of financial knowledge. The cost of a degree in America is ridiculously high. For example, the costs of an Associate degree are roughly $25,000, Bachelor's degree is $35,000, and a Master's degree is $40,00 and up. The cost of a college degree will vary according to in-state tuition, living expenses, and the college/university fees for their programs.

In life, there are no free rides with anything. Earning a college degree will cost you time with studying, hard work, determination, and money. To invest in the stock market, it will also cost you time to read and analyze various factors in the market, hard work, determination, money, etc.

I am not writing this book to enforce you to invest in the stock market. I am providing an option for you to invest in the stock market in your lifetime. This option was not provided to me as a child. I learned about the stock market in my 30's. What is the cost and benefits of not investing in the stock market? What are the costs and benefits of investing in the stock market? When a person decides on something, you must understand the value of it and the benefits from receiving it. Also, in life, you have a decision to stay in your current situation or change it. The choice is yours.

Remember, investing in the stock market is not based on your emotions. You have to boss up and aggressively take back all the years that was stolen from your life by negative thinking, poor money management skills, and lack of investment. You are worthy to live a financially free lifestyle. You are worthy to learn about the stock market and start small if you need to. You are worthy to live a life on purpose and have what you desire. The bottom line is negative thinking alter your emotions and leads to poor behavior.

Evaluate your current situation. What has negative thinking done for you? Changing your thought process from negative to positive is essential when investing in anything. The best part of investing in the stock market and the cost of it is the benefits of meeting your financial goals. Okay, there are some individuals who are opportunistic about the benefits in the stock market, but despite this, we must still be determined to ride this financial freedom process out until the end. Knowledge is power and grants us access to the investment world.

If you want to start small, start with as little as $5.00 with discount investment firms such as Stash or Acorns. Both investment apps are geared to assist beginners to invest in the stock market. One tip to follow when selecting any investment company is to analyze their management fees, portfolio options, advisors, training tools, account minimums, promotions, trading fees, and account types. Another tip is to identify the timeframe you would like to invest, your risk level, and investment strategy as mentioned in a previous chapter, and consider your goals.

A working person should invest his money in the future. You can grow your money when investing it into stocks, bonds, real estate, and other investment securities. Some things to consider when you are purchasing a stock are companies that you are passionate about. Which talents or hobbies do you have? Which companies do you spend your money on? Evaluate the growth of the company. There are several types of portfolios and investments you can select.

As an investor, you can purchase Traditional IRA, Roth IRA, bond or bond funds, index funds, mutual funds, exchange-traded funds, or stocks. Make sure to examine your investment style to select the right type of investment. A tip you should always remember is there is no unique investment style.

Why should you invest in the stock market? When you discover your *why* that's when your "real" investment journey starts. As a single parent, I decided to seek after financial freedom in a way that has never been done in my family's history. I do understand that I desire to break through the financial industry and investment is one of those methods. It is not about me.

I started on my investment journey after I discovered my *why*. After I was able to answer my *why*, I realized investing in my future, children, and teaching investment strategies to my circle of influence was a must. You can commit to change negative habits and adopt new ones. I have no desire for my children to experience some of the things I have in my life. It is about my children, teaching and mentoring others, and creating a legacy.

I said all of that to say, why shouldn't I invest? I decided investing would create a financial lifestyle I dreamed about. You should invest in the stock market because of your legacy. At this very moment, what do you have to leave your children if you pass away? Will you leave them bills and debt or a legacy to carry on? The stock market is one avenue among many investment opportunities to achieve your financial goals. If you came from a family with little or no investment education, this can be one of your reasons why you should invest in the stock market. I believe investing takes courage.

Individuals invest their money to grow it, to enroll in college, purchase a car, for retirement, financial freedom, create a business, assist other people, or start a new venture. I want you to be excited about your new journey and not run away from it. Investing in the stock market does not have to be a long drawn out process. If you can save money in your local bank, you can invest in the stock market. It is essential to know yourself when investing. Knowing yourself can determine your investment styles and goals. I have listed twelve critical tips to help you along your investment journey.

- Check your emotions.
- Don't lose money.
- Always selected a stock that you are similar with such as a product you use on a daily basis.
- Understand your risk tolerance.
- Be patient when you purchase a stock.
- Do your homework.
- Do not purchase a stock because your friends or family members have.
- Make sure you select an entrance and exit plan.
- Re-evaluate your investment plan as your financial goals change.
- Persistence is a key to investment success.
- Be patient.
- Read.

You see, there is no one size fit them all solution when investing in the stock market. The secret to success is to start somewhere.

ABOUT THE AUTHOR

Delia Williams, M.S., is also the author of *The Adventures of Zechariah and the Money Machine*, a cutting-edge children's book that teaches children how to invest in the stock market in a fun, childlike way. She is a financial educator who teaches individuals to understand the stock market simply. She has taught locally and over social media outlets on financial literacy and investments. Born in Fayetteville, NC, Delia now lives in Charlotte, NC, with her three children: Tanihya, Zechariah, and Mackenzie. Delia is the founder of D & T Investment and Consultant, Single Moms & Stocks, LLC., and Dot's Naturals, LLC.

www.ingramcontent.com/pod-product-compliance
Lightning Source LLC
Chambersburg PA
CBHW031542210526
45464CB00003B/1106